DBT Workbook

Fun & Practical Dialectal Behavior Therapy Skills Training For Children

Help Kids Recognize Their Emotions, Manage Anxiety & Phobias, and Learn To Thrive!

By Barrett Huang

https://barretthuang.com/

1

The following book is reproduced below to provide information that is as accurate and reliable as possible. Regardless, purchasing this book can be seen as consent to the fact that both the publisher and the author are not experts on the topics discussed within and that any recommendations or suggestions made herein are for entertainment purposes only. Professionals should be consulted as needed before undertaking any actions endorsed herein.

This declaration is deemed fair and valid by the American Bar Association and the Committee of Publishers Association, thus making it legally binding throughout the United States.

Furthermore, the transmission, duplication, or reproduction of any of the following work, including specific information, will be considered illegal, whether done electronically or in print. This extends to creating a secondary or tertiary copy of the work or a recorded copy and is only allowed with express written consent from the Publisher. All additional rights reserved.

The information in the following pages is broadly considered a truthful and accurate account of facts. As such, any inattention, use, or misuse of the

FREE Guide:

Mastering DBT Essentials

FREE DOWNLOAD ALERT!

Master Dialectical Behavior Therapy Skills in 5 Simple Steps with my Free DBT Quick Guide. Access the 'Mastering DBT Essentials' quick guide at:

https://barretthuang.com/dbt-quick-guide/

Or scan the code below:

Table of Contents

FREE Guide: 4

Introduction 8

   For Parents... 9

Worry Cloud 10

Safe Place Meditation 11

Chapter One: What is "wrong" with me? 13

   Quick Assessment 22

   Definitions 24

Calm Fun 27

Wordsearch 29

   What is DBT? 38

Yoga 40

Drawing and Coloring 41

I Spy... 42

Chapter Three: Basics of Boundaries 43

   Assessment 50

Action Plan 54

I am/I am not 56

My Boundaries 58

Chapter Four: Anxiety and Worry 59

   Quick Assessment 66

   Anxiety 67

DBT Toolbox 69

The Wise Mind Web...73

Mindfulness..75

    Quick Assessment...84

    ADD and the H..85

Make A Routine...86

Interpersonal Effectiveness....................................90

Drawing for Calm...92

Chapter Six: Phobias...93

    Phobias...100

Phobias Worksheet...101

Distress Tolerance..103

    ACCEPTS...103

Radical Acceptance..105

The Worry Jar...107

Chapter Seven: PTSD, Panic Disorder and Agoraphobia...........109

    Quick Assessment..116

    PTSD, Panic, and Agoraphobia - What is it?..............117

    Agoraphobia...118

Self Soothe...119

Emotion Regulation..120

Stop, Look, Listen..122

Chapter Eight: OCD, Compulsive Behaviours and Body-Focused Repetitive Behaviours...123

    Quick Assessment..130

    What is OCD?..131

Body-Focused Repetitive Behaviours 132

The OCD Monster 133

Thought —> Action 135

Matching 136

Chapter Nine: Selective Mutism 137

Quick Assessment 144

What is Selective mutism? 145

What makes you nervous? 146

Telephone 148

Dare List 149

Chapter Ten: For Parents 150

Getting Involved 150

Validation 150

Positive and Negative Behaviours 151

Final Thoughts 155

Review Request 156

Further Reading 157

About the Author 160

Resources 161

Introduction

Hi!

Will you do something with me? Take a nice deep breath. Start from way down in your belly. As you breathe in, imagine your stomach is like a balloon filling up with air. Good! Now, hold it... hold it... hold it! Alright, let it out slowly through your nose.

Feel any better?

It's so easy to get overwhelmed and feel like you're standing in the middle of a swirling hurricane, can't it? You might feel like you don't have much say in things, or you might feel like school, family, sports, or clubs are making you dizzy, and your tummy hurts.

You might feel like you can't breathe sometimes because there's *too much.*

I want to tell you something: you aren't alone! Many of the kids in your class, school, or neighbour might feel the same way. And you know what? That's okay. You're okay. Even when it feels like things are out of control, you are alright.

This workbook will help you take a step back from those feelings that seem to tighten your chest or make the world spin. Those feelings you're having are called anxiety. And by working in this book, you're taking steps toward controlling anxiety rather than letting it control you. And also, you'll probably have some fun!

The chapters in this book will cover anxiety, Dialectic Behavior Therapy, Boundaries, ADD/ADHD, Phobias, PTSD, Selective Mutism and OCD.

You can think of anxiety-like a dragon to slay, a tough skateboard trick, or a tough dance move. To own and control it, you have to practice and keep practising to stay sharp.

I believe in you. I know your parents and teachers do. Now, take that deep breath, and believe in yourself, too.

For Parents...

Big feelings can be a lot for anyone to deal with, especially for children whose minds are still forming. Try to remember what it was like for you as a kid. So much is going on, yet so much is expected of you. Everything is scary or exciting, but mostly just overwhelming. It's helping your child work through the feeling of overwhelming stimulation that can aid in feelings of anxiety. Learning to cope with anxiety early means that your child will be better equipped to handle all the stresses of adult life. Taking these steps now encouraging practice means that your child will understand their anxiety and be able to use coping practices to relieve stresses and support meditation and health.

Worry Cloud

Write your name in the center cloud. Then, write the things that are giving you anxiety right now in the surrounding circles. It could be worrying that you won't do well on a school project, being anxious about fire safety, or being unsure about a new food.

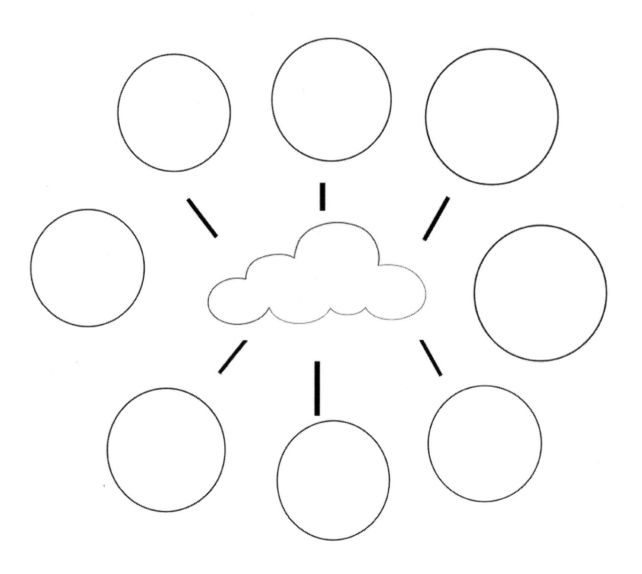

Safe Place Meditation

You've got a great imagination, don't you? Well, it's time to use it! Read over the instructions below.

I want you to imagine a place you feel safe. It can be your room, a favourite camping spot, a fantasy world in a book or movie, or even the comfiest spot on the couch. Maybe there are people you love there, too.

Let your whole body relax, starting with the tips of your toes and working your way up to the top of your head. Remind yourself that you are safe, loved, and happy here. This is your safe space, a place you can go anytime.

Chapter One: What is "wrong" with me?

"The greatest weapon against stress is our ability to choose one thought over another."

~William James

This is Tibby, the cat! Tibby lives with
her mother and father, and brother, Zip.
Tibby goes to school down the road.

Often, Tibby gets nervous. Her paws get sweaty, her face gets hot, and she gets worried about leaving the house. Her parents expect a lot from her because they want her to do well. Her little brother always needs her help. There is so much to do for school

Tibby worries. She feels anxious and scared.
More and more, she finds that the safest place is at
home under the covers in her room.
There, she's safe, and no one wants anything from her.
But there are a hundred things that Tibby needs to look
after outside her room. It feels like too much.

But one day, Tibby's mum came into her room.
She brought a workbook.
"Something to help clear your mind and help you
take a deep breath." Her mum said.
Tibby reached a hand out from under the covers
and pulled the workbook in.
It was full ofactivities, images, and words to
help her cope.

Under the covers, Tibby gave a little smile.
Maybe she could start to feel better, after all.

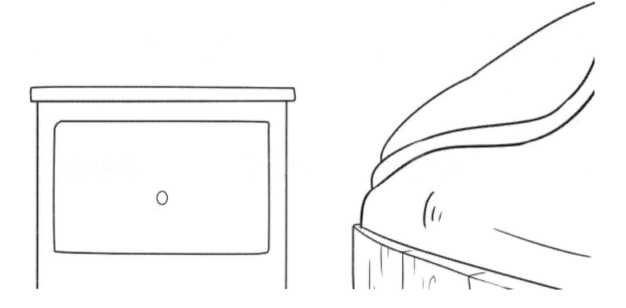

What happens to Tibby's body when she gets nervous?

Where does Tibby think is the safest place?

What does Tibby's Mum give her?

Quick Assessment

This is a question that can be tough to ask. But know that it's got an easy answer. Nothing.

There is nothing "wrong" with you at all. Take that in for a moment. Repeat it. There is nothing wrong with you.

Everyone gets scared or nervous, but it can really take hold of some of us. Anxiety and DBT can be really tough to live with. But that does not mean there is any problem with you or your actions. But you can do something to make yourself feel better and more at ease. Starting with this workbook!

Firstly, let's see how you've been coping with all the stresses of life. Below, there are a few questions. Don't worry; there is no "wrong" answer! This test is just to see how you're doing and if this book is right for you.

Rate each of the below questions on a scale of 0 (not at all) to 3 (very much)

Recently (within the last week, for example), have you...

   a) Felt nervous?
   b) Felt as if you aren't in control of whatever situation you're in?
   c) Had trouble relaxing?
   d) Been so restless that it's challenging to sit still?
   e) Felt afraid or fearful?
   f) Worried something terrible might happen?
   g) Become annoyed easily?

Scoring

   - 0 to 4 = mild anxiety
   - 5 to 9 = moderate anxiety
   - 10 to 14 = moderately severe anxiety
   - 15 to 21 = severe anxiety

Try to keep in mind that even if the score is not what you wanted. It is okay, and you are doing the best you can. This workbook will help you find ways to help deal with your anxiety.

Definitions

Now, let's work on defining some of these strange words. The better you understand the terms and definitions, the better you can understand what is happening in your mind. These words will be used in the workbook.

Generalized anxiety disorder: an emotion or feeling of worry, nervousness, and unease, often showing as symptoms such as trouble breathing regularly, dizziness, or wanting to throw up.

Separation anxiety disorder: having anxiety or severe stress about leaving home or being away from family members or friends

Social Anxiety: having anxiety or severe stress about being around people or situations involving talking and meeting with people.

Health Anxiety: having anxiety or severe stress about your health and body.

ADD/ADHD: Attention Deficit Disorder, or attention deficit hyperactivity disorder, has symptoms like difficulty paying attention, impulsive behavior, self-control, and attention span.

Panic Disorders: conditions where you might feel trapped, fearful, or scared. Panic attacks can feel very scary and come on quickly, including a flash of heat, increased heart rate, fear, and physical reactions, even though there is no present physical danger.

PTSD (Post Traumatic Stress Disorder): the emotional and mental response that develops after some people have had shocking, traumatic, scary, or dangerous events in their lives.

Specific Phobias: the intense and irrational fear of something that does not actually pose any real danger to you and brings anxiety when faced with it or thinking about it.

OCD (Obsessive Compulsive Disorder): an anxiety disorder that shows itself as uncontrollable and recurring thoughts (obsessions) and behaviors (compulsions).

Body-Focused Repetitive Behaviors: body behaviours that include hair pulling, nail-biting, and skin picking.

Selective mutism: an anxiety disorder where a person cannot speak in certain social situations, such as in a classroom or with strangers.

DBT (Dialectical Behaviour Therapy): a therapy that helps relieve feelings of anxiety through mindfulness and acceptance.

Stress: mental or emotional worry and strain

Meditation: thinking carefully and gently on a subject to bring peace and calm

Mindfulness: a mental state that happens when you focus on the current moment and breathe in and out while thinking, acknowledging, and accepting your feelings and thoughts.

Calm: a soothing feeling of relaxation and peace, a lack of tension or worry in the current moment. Maybe when you watch your favorite show.

Personal Boundaries: a set of values you honor and defend to protect your mental health and wellbeing. Having a boundary means when something makes you uncomfortable, you stop doing it.

You don't have to memorize these definitions, but it's a great idea to get a sense of them and understand them. Oftentimes, the first step toward overcoming something that troubles you is understanding it.

Calm Fun

Find the centre of the mazes. Take your time and have fun.

Wordsearch

Wordsearch

I	N	T	E	R	P	E	R	S	O	N	A	L	R
T	Y	E	A	C	C	E	P	T	A	N	C	E	E
H	Y	P	E	R	A	C	T	I	V	I	T	Y	R
W	N	M	I	N	D	F	U	L	N	E	S	S	O
A	O	B	R	E	A	T	H	E	D	T	I	D	I
N	I	R	B	O	U	N	D	A	R	I	E	S	V
X	E	A	R	R	E	L	A	X	P	R	X	I	A
I	I	E	E	Y	Y	A	N	H	U	A	C	A	H
E	B	N	U	O	P	T	O	M	I	S	M	I	E
T	T	E	S	N	E	R	V	O	U	S	M	B	B
Y	D	I	S	T	R	E	S	S	P	S	L	O	A
P	A	N	I	C	S	C	A	R	E	D	A	H	P
V	M	E	D	I	T	A	T	I	O	N	C	P	D
A	P	E	A	C	E	F	U	L	I	S	A	F	E

MINDFULNESS
PHOBIA
ACCEPTANCE
WORRY
HYPERACTIVITY
INTERPERSONAL
BEHAVIOR
DISTRESS
OPTOMISM
BREATHE
SCARED
NERVOUS
RELAX
SAFE
BOUNDARIES
PEACEFUL
PANIC
ANXIETY
CALM
MEDITATION

Play this puzzle online at : https://thewordsearch.com/puzzle/3259487/

Chapter Two: The Basics of DBT

"You're braver than you believe and stronger than you seem, and smarter than you think."

~Christopher Robin

This is Zip, the cat! He is Tibby's brother. Zip has some trouble sometimes with his mindset.
He doesn't like eating because it makes him nervous.
What will it do, the food that goes into his belly?
What if he overeats?
What if he doesn't like how he looks?
Zip has a hard time eating. He will just push his food around his plate most nights. He is often hungry but doesn't want to let himself eat because he doesn't like the feel of the food in his mouth.

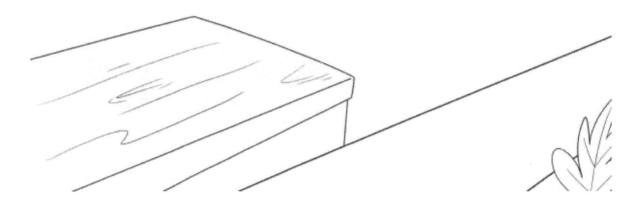

But then his Dad helped him learn about DBT.
This therapy could help him retake control of his
feelings. It could help him accept and be mindful to
help move past some of the things
he has a hard time with.

Zip is learning, and though it might be slow or hard,
he keeps going. Change doesn't happen overnight!
It's putting in the effort that counts.
Zip is more than worth it.

How is Zip the Cat related to Tibby?

_____

What does eating make Zip feel?

_____

Does Zip like the feeling of food in his mouth?

_____

What is DBT?

In DBT, mindfulness is the key. Getting to the bottom of what is bothering you, meditating on it, sitting with it, and then accepting it. DBT is a cognitive behavioral therapy focusing on the mind and our thoughts about our traumas and anxieties.

The Tools of DBT can be used when you feel anxious, nervous, scared or worried. They can help you feel calmer and more in control of your emotions and reactions.

Mindfulness

It is being aware of your thoughts and feelings. You notice your feelings and let them be there.

Interpersonal Effectiveness

Our relationship with others can make how we feel about ourselves, better or worse. If we are happy in how we treat and get along with others, we are happy in how we treat ourselves.

Distress Tolerance

Make sure that our worries don't get us filled up with anger or fear by noticing our fears and worries.

Emotion Regulation

Learning to understand our feelings and when to act on them.

Yoga

Grab a parent and get them to help you bring up YouTube on a computer, phone, or tablet. Search for "kids yoga videos". Pick one you like, and get it all set up. The activity will last as long as the video, so if you're looking for a reasonable time frame for kids, pick a video between 5-10 minutes.

To make you comfier, use a rug or a yoga mat in a place you love that's calm and quiet, and bring a bottle of water. Get comfortable, relax, and focus on the following along with the video. Physical exercise is a great way to connect with your body and yourself, and yoga helps to promote deep breathing and feeling centered.

Drawing and Coloring

Draw a picture of yourself below. Show how you're feeling right now by colouring it in. Red for angry, yellow for happy, green for anxious, or whatever color means something to you.

I Spy...

Can you spot things that match the descriptions? It's not a race but a fun way to notice everything around you. Slow down and see if you can spot everything on the list from where you're sitting. When you do spot something on the list, check it off!

☐ something made of paper (your workbook!)

☐ something green

☐ something soft

☐ something made of wood

☐ something you love

☐ something that makes you laugh

☐ something with a tail

☐ something that would tickle you

☐ something you can pick up with one hand

Chapter Three: Basics of Boundaries

"Courage is not the absence of fear, but doing something despite fear."

~Unknown

Tibby has had a tiring day at school.
There were lots of sounds and sights
and people talking. All she wants to do
is rest in her room and take a minute
to enjoy the quiet.

But her brother Zip keeps coming into her room,
even though her door is closed. He keeps asking to play.
But Tibby just needs some quiet time for twenty minutes.

Tibby loves her brother. She does not want to
hurt his feelings. Zip isn't doing anything wrong;
it's just that Tibby is not ready to play yet.
Tibby knows she has to set her boundaries.

When Zip comes in without knocking again, Tibby tells him that she will play with him and that she likes playing with him. But for a few minutes, she needs to be alone. She tells him that she will come to find him soon when she is ready. And once he leaves the room, she closes her door and locks it.

What is all Tibby wants to do when she gets home from school?

What does Zip want Tibby to do?

What does Tibby tell Zip she needs?

Assessment

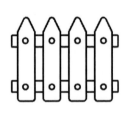 Let's talk a little about creating boundaries. What does that mean? Well, a boundary is like a roadblock. Boundaries help you figure out how far you're willing to be pushed. Below is a little survey; simply answer yes or no to each question. And remember, there are no wrong answers or incorrect outcomes! Just take a breath and be honest.

1. I often say yes to others, even when I want to say no.
2. I always put others' needs before my own.
3. I forget that my thoughts and opinions are just as important as anyone else's.
4. I find myself giving in when someone pesters me about something

5. Somehow, I ended up unhappy when all I tried to do was make others happy

If you said yes to most of the sentences, you likely need to create some emotional boundaries. Now, this doesn't mean that you're putting up walls! Emotional or real.

Setting boundaries means that we respect ourselves and our own time. It is good to be friendly, thoughtful, and helpful to others. But we cannot fill others' cups if our own is empty. Creating emotional boundaries means finding and knowing your limits. It's not going to be the same for everyone, and that is okay! Some people might need to have boundaries on their social time with family or friends. Some might require boundaries regarding how much they can give in a project or a club.

Boundaries are a form of taking care of yourself to keep being kind and caring for others.

Some places where you might need to make boundaries include...

Home:

 Homelife between parents, siblings, relatives, chores, responsibilities, and pets can be mentally exhausting. Limiting family time is okay if you feel it is hurting you mentally. Limiting can mean going to your room for quiet time, a walk, or a friend's.

Or perhaps certain topics of conversation that family members push on you make you uncomfortable. It's okay to set boundaries or agree to disagree.

School:

 Perhaps you might feel that you need boundaries with personal vs school life with classmates. Maybe your teachers want a lot from you because they know you're capable. That's great to have confidence in you, and putting in the effort is important. Still, it doesn't mean that you are obligated to run yourself ragged in the name of getting a perfect score on a test.

World:

 Friends might want to spend time with you outside the classroom. That's great! But remember that you can say no sometimes, and it won't hurt your friendship, especially if you explain that you may just need a quiet evening to relax.

Digital World:

 An important place to set boundaries is the digital world of social media. You could put a time limit on your screen time or perhaps a posting per week limit to help you spend less time on your phone. Social media is a world of fake perfection, and it oftentimes pretends that everything is great when it may not be. Don't forget that everyone behind their phone is a real person, just like you.

With Self:

 Boundaries with the self can take the form of being mindful of toxic thoughts or limiting time being hard on yourself until you realize that you don't have to be. You might sometimes put yourself down, call yourself names or think you can't get anything right. But it's so important to speak kindly to yourself and treat yourself like you would a good friend.

Action Plan

One of the most important things you can do to set boundaries is writing them down. Make yourself a list, and check it every day before you sleep or when you first wake up. Make these thought patterns and behavioral patterns your habit. Setting boundaries means respecting and honoring yourself. You'll find that your relationships improve, or the bad ones for you fall away. And that's okay. Protecting your wellbeing is one of the most important things you can do as you grow up because it means building the foundation for a positive, healthy life moving forward.

Create your action plan. Write down the places where you think you might need to set boundaries in your life. There are no wrong answers or wrong moves. Think about the situations in your life where you aren't as happy. Where do you think that comes from? What would you do to make your life a little more positive? Maybe limiting how much time you spend on homework without a break.

I am/I am not

Fill in the rest of the sentences below. Remember that there are no wrong answers!

X

*I am not*_____*stupid*_____

I am not

_____

I do not

_____

I will not

_____

I am_____ smart_____.

I am

_____

I will

_____

I do

_____

My Boundaries

Fill in the squares with the boundaries you will set at school, in the world, in the digital world, at home, and with yourself. Examples might be setting a time limit of 30 minutes after school on-screen time.

WORLD	
HOME	
SELF	
SCHOOL	
DIGITAL WORLD	

Chapter Four: Anxiety and Worry

"When you're feeling anxious, remember that you're still you. You are not your anxiety."

~Deanne Repich

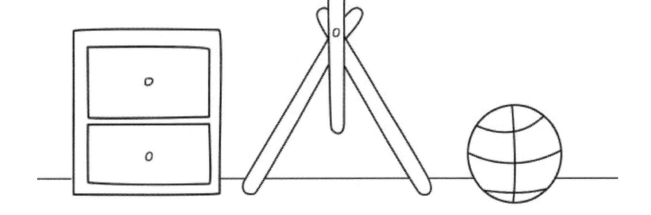

Zip, the cat, can't stop worrying about a project for school. He has to speak in front of his class. He does not like the sound of it.

Zip feels a terrible feeling in his belly whenever he remembers the project.

He feels sweaty and scared. He wonders if he can pretend to be sick to get out of the project.

His big sister Tibby noticed Zip acting funny. She asked him what was wrong, and after a little, Zip told her. Tibby nodded. She understood why Zip was nervous and scared. She remembered doing the project herself last year. She tells Zip this.

"Zip, I was scared when I had to talk in front of my class, too. A lot of kids are. But that's okay. It can be a good learning experience to do things that scare you."

"Yeah, but I'm still nervous!" Zip said.

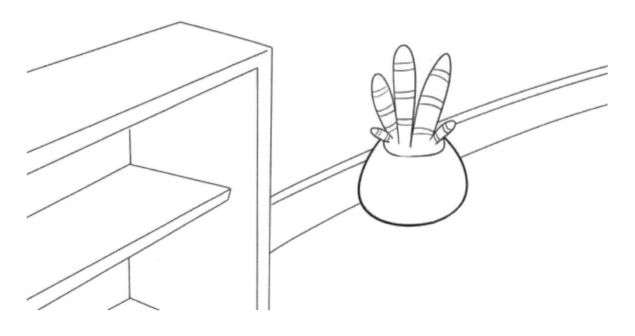

Tibby nodded. "The best thing to do is to
practice, practice, practice. And remember
that everyone else is nervous, too.
You aren't alone. And the people you have
to talk in front of are your friends,
and they understand how hard it is too."
Zip thought about that.
"You're right. I'm still nervous, but I feel like
I can do it now, because I won't be the only one."

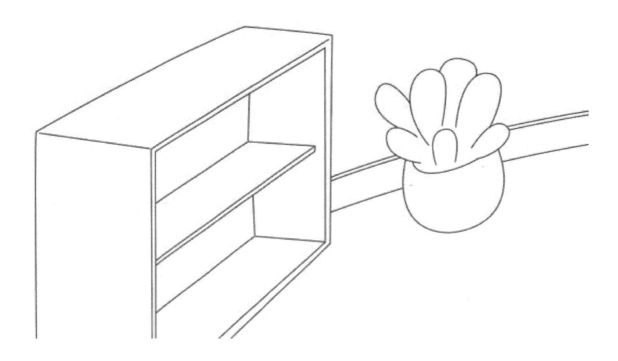

What was Zip worried about for school?

_____

Where does Zip feel the terrible feeling in his body?

_____

Tibby said the best thing to do is...?

_____

Quick Assessment

Have you recently felt...

- Worried?
- Scared?
- Unsure of what to do?
- So queasy you might throw up?
- Sweaty and clammy?
- Frightened for what might happen next?
- Jumpy and unsettled?
- Like you want to run away?

If you feel any of those things, it's okay. We're all allowed to feel scared sometimes. Everyone gets scared and nervous, even if they are good at hiding it.

One thing to remember is that everyone gets worried. Being worried means you care and think through all the things that might happen. This can keep you safe sometimes, reminding you to think about what you are doing.

But the tough part comes when the worry and anxiety start taking over your day. Most of the time, being anxious is very tiring, mentally and physically. You need to live a balanced life, be cautious at times and enjoy life, too!

Anxiety

What is it?

Anxiety can make you scared or fearful, but it might also make you mad or upset. Anxiety is when your emotions are unbalanced, and worry and fear take over. You might have trouble sleeping or get a queasy tummy because something makes you nervous or you are worried about an event, school, or project.

It's important to share with a parent, sibling, or trusted teacher when you are feeling anxious because they will help you balance out how you're feeling again.

So, what are the different types of anxiety? Let's take a look...

Generalized Anxiety: having worry or fear about something that gets in the way of your everyday life. You might have trouble sleeping, restlessness, worry, trembling, sweating, anger, or fear for a long time, over weeks or months.

Separation Anxiety: fear of being away from someone or people you have grown attached to. This could be your Mom or Dad or your friends. You feel like you can not be relaxed or happy at all unless you are close to that person.

Social Anxiety: being afraid or fearful of being around other people or having to talk or hang out with them. Can be worried about what to say, how to respond, or just act. You could be concerned about something like going to a new school or meeting people your age.

Health Anxiety: worrying about getting sick, germs, and being unwell. Germs can be spread from things like toilet seats or door handles. Washing your hands well with soap and water makes sure that the germs can't be passed around.

DBT Toolbox

This is your DBT toolbox! Just like a real toolbox, this worksheet will help you find the right tool for dealing with anxiety and worry.

Square Breathing

Breathe in for 4 seconds, hold for 4, breathe out for 4, hold for 4, and then begin again. Breathing helps calm you and tells your body everything will be alright. Getting air into your lungs slowly and on purpose also helps slow down the responses of your body that might signal anxiety. Imagine your breath like a square, up to one side (breathing in for 4), across the top (hold for 4), down the other side (out for 4) and then along the bottom (hold for 4).

Radical Acceptance

 Accept something for what it is, no matter how hard to swallow. Something might be out of your control. You can't control everything. Notice that it is not for you to solve it, just accept it. A good way to do this is:

Take in a deep breath. Think about the thing that is making you anxious. Think about what it is and how it affects your life. Does it make going to school hard? Or does it make you sad? Tell yourself that you can't change it. You can only accept it.

Ride the Wave

 Feel your feelings. Notice how they make you feel. But don't react to them. Just ride the wave of your emotions and let them wash over you. Here's what this looks like:

Go somewhere you're comfortable. Think about the thing that's bothering you, and let all your emotions and feelings about it rise. Concentrate on them. Feel your feelings. Don't push them away. Let yourself feel, and then take a deep breath.

Failing Forward

 Failing at something doesn't have to be a bad thing. It can be the turning point. Let yourself learn from your mistakes to understand how to do things. Think about the times when something didn't go as well as you hoped it would. Notice what lessons you learned from failing; notice how you've grown as a person since then.

Moment to Pause

 Take a breath, and see how you feel. Let everything stop for a minute. No one needs or wants anything from you at this moment. Just take a moment to breathe. Breath deeply, in and out. Notice that you do not have to do anything at all other than breathe right now.

Learned Optimism

 Learned Optimism means choosing to feel optimistic and joyful about the future. Everyone can be happy and optimistic, but it is something that should be practiced. Like any skill, practice makes perfect, and when you do something over and over again, it becomes a habit. Optimism can be your habit!

Learned Optimism focuses on good thoughts and noticing thoughts that make you feel bad. These bad thoughts, or negative self-talk, are something to look for and stop when you see them.

Wise Mind

 A wise Mind is a place of wisdom. Wisdom knows something, and the thing you know is usually known because you've learned a lesson. When our hearts (what we feel) and our heads (what we think) come together, this gives us the best way forward.

When we use our Wise Mind, we use the best parts of our thinking and feeling to develop a great solution.

An example of using your Wise Mind might be taking a few minutes of quiet time to reflect when you are in a fight or upset with someone. These few moments allow you to sit and feel all your feelings, but then let you think about your feelings and see how the other person might be feeling, too. This reflection means that your thoughts and emotions have a chance to balance and help you see your truth.

The Wise Mind Web

Below is the Wise Mind Web. The Feeling mind means being led by your feelings. The Thinking mind means making choices based on your thoughts. The Wise mind brings both together for a balance of mind and heart.

Fill in the bubbles with what you think falls under each. What do you do that might go in the feeling mind bubble? The Thinking mind bubble? And, most importantly, the wise mind bubble. There are a few examples below.

Feeling mind - *I'm mad at my friend so that I won't listen to them*
Wise mind - *I'll talk with my friend, we will solve our problem together.*
Thinking mind - *I'll ignore my feelings and do what my friend wants.*

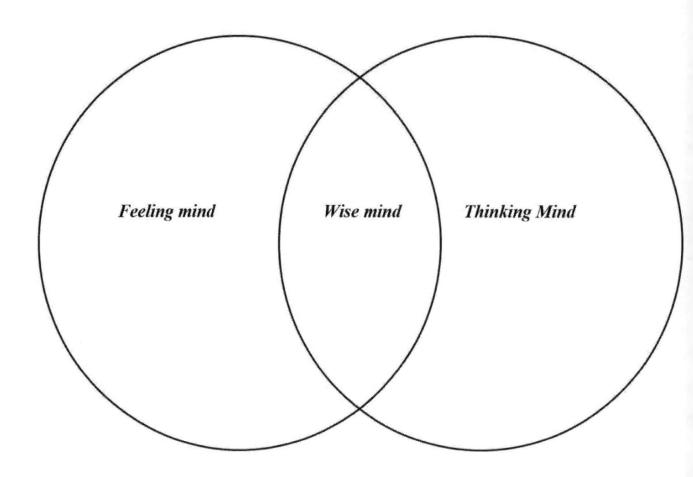

Which bubble do you think is best to use when you're upset or mad?

Which one do you think would make you happiest?

Mindfulness

 Mindfulness is paying attention at the moment to your body, your thoughts, and your feelings. It is slowing down to notice what is going on within you. It can make you feel peaceful, happy, or even sad. Whatever your inner feelings are, you can figure them out with a little bit of mindfulness.

1. Get comfortable and make sure you'll be warm

2. Close your eyes. Breathe in deeply and slowly.

3. Starting with your toes, relax your body, moving all the way up to your face.

4. Now, think of something you love. It can be a person, a place, or even a thing.

5. Imagine the thing you love. What it looks like, what it sounds like, what it feels like.

6. How does it make you feel?

7. Slowly open your eyes.

8. On the lines below, write down what you felt.

Chapter Five: ADD and ADHD

"Don't underestimate the value of doing nothing, of just going along, listening to all the things you can't hear, and not bothering."

~Winnie the Pooh

Tibby, the cat, has trouble sitting still.
She often feels restless, and can't seem to focus
on one thought at a time. She went to her room
today to get something for her mum, but then
noticed that her pet fish might be hungry,
and so she went to the shelf
where she keeps the food.

But then she saw her journal, and opened it,
remembering that she was supposed to write down
a reflection entry for school.

And for that, she would need a pen.
So Tibby turned to her desk and opened the drawer.
There, she spotted a postcard from her friend when she
went away on vacation, which made her remember that
she had been making a friendship bracelet for her
friend, so she went over to the basket of beads...

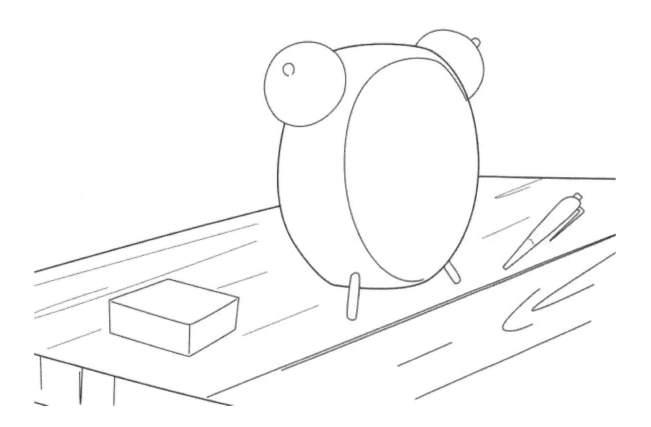

"Tibby? Did you find your laundry basket?"
Oops! That was what Tibby was supposed to be doing!
Well, now she remembered.

How does Tibby often feel?

_____

Why does she keep her journal?

_____

What was she supposed to write down?

_____

What was she making for her friend?

_____

Quick Assessment

Answer the questions below. These are some of the signs that you might have ADD/ADHD.

- Do you find it hard to pay attention?
- Do you have trouble keeping things neat and tidy?
- Are you forgetful?
- Do you struggle to sit still?
- Do you often lose things?

- Have a hard time following instructions?
- Do you talk a lot?
- Do you feel like you need to be constantly moving?
- Do you struggle to be quiet?

Don't forget! Just because you answered yes to the questions does not mean you have ADHD. Talk to a parent and psychiatrist.

ADD and the H

The H in ADHD stands for Hyperactivity. This means that you are very high energy and always need to be moving, moving, moving. But the thing is, you probably don't have a goal or task in mind. You just need to fidget, move around, and maybe talk a lot and quickly.

Hyperactivity means you have trouble with slow, quiet tasks and don't like sitting still. This can make learning in a classroom hard because sometimes classroom learning needs students to be quiet, listen, and sit still.

Make A Routine

A routine can help make you feel under control, safe, and good. Knowing exactly what is coming up next can help you feel calm and prepared.

Doing the same thing at the same time every day is a routine. It could be waking up, having breakfast, brushing your teeth, and getting dressed.

- Think about the crucial steps in your day. What would you like to put into your routine? Is there anything that you would like to start doing?
- Write it down with a grownup, and put it somewhere you can see. Maybe next to your bed or in the bathroom mirror.
- Make sure that there are fun things in your routine, too—time for playing, relaxing, or watching TV.
- It's okay if it's hard when you first start. A routine takes time to learn and get used to. Don't be hard on yourself!
- Don't forget that you can always change your routine if something isn't working or the seasons change. Perhaps you want to go to bed a little later in the summertime, but you want to add time to play in the snow in the winter.

Here's an example of a routine if you need some help!

Morning: fold my blanket, brush my teeth, wash my face, eat breakfast, get dressed

Afternoon: eat lunch, go for a walk, play with my little brother

Evening: have dinner, watch a TV show, brush my teeth, put away my toys from the day

Bedtime: read a story, get into bed

Please fill in the chart below with your routine!

Morning
Afternoon
Evening
Night

This is all about how you get on with others. Do you share, have manners, and speak kindly? Can you see things from someone else's point of view? It means balancing your wants and needs with others' wants and needs.

Getting along well with others is a learned skill. Being fair and kind and seeing what's best for everyone is a great way to make friends and keep things calm and happy.

The way we treat others is a reflection of how we treat ourselves. Understanding the balance between doing what's good for others and what is good for you is important.

Fill in the table below with Y or N for Yes or No, and say why.

Interpersonal Effectiveness

What is Interpersonal Effectiveness?

To have good Interpersonal Effectiveness, I should...	Y/N	Why?
Listen well by looking at the speaker	Y	To show them I am listening & connected
Fidget or play with something while someone talks		
Use good manners and eye contact		
Avoid talking to people and cross my arms in front		

of me		
Not eat all the cookies myself, even though they're yummy		

Drawing for Calm

When you think of the seashore, what do you imagine? Crabs and seagulls, or maybe lots and lots of sand? Or perhaps you think about the waves, boats, or the sunset.

Think of the seashore, keeping in mind all the calming parts about it. Soft sand, the sound of waves on the beach, or the pleasant warmth of the sun. Draw all the things on the seashore that calm you below.

Chapter Six: Phobias

"When everything seems to be going against you, remember that the airplane takes off against the wind, not with it."

~Henry Ford

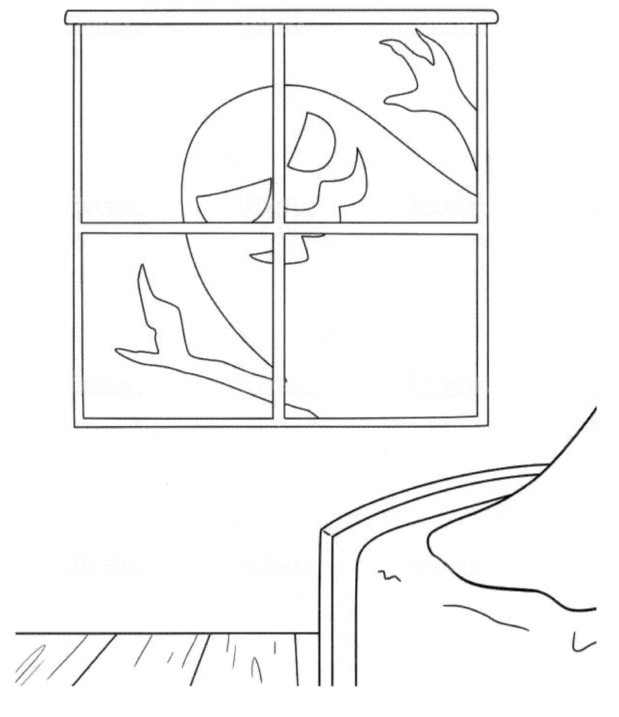

Zip, the cat, seems to be afraid of everything. But his worst fear is the dark. Zip does not like going to bed sometimes, because he is afraid. He lies awake at night, unable to sleep because he can't see everything around him, and he's unsure if there is some scary monster.

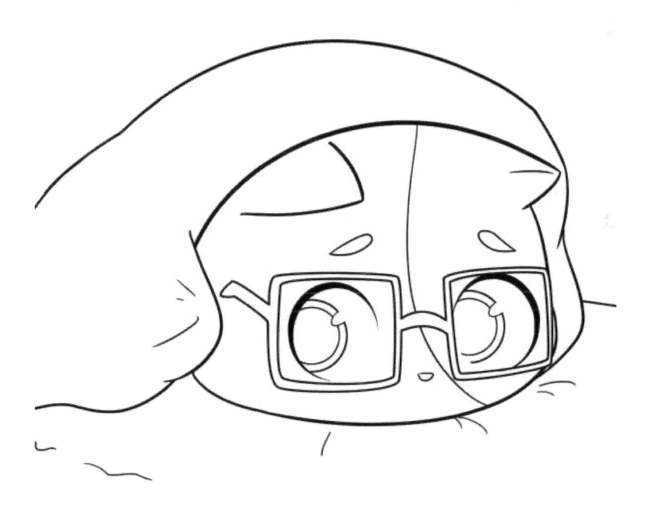

When he goes to school, he is tired and grouchy.
He gets mad at his friends and teachers because he is so
tired and grumpy.

When he gets home, he falls asleep on the couch
before dinner. His Dad notices that he is always tired.

"Why haven't you been sleeping, Zip?" He asks.

"I'm... afraid. I'm too scared to sleep."

His dad thinks about this for a minute.

"I have a few ideas to help you." He says.

They find Tibby's old nightlight and plug it into Zip's room. Now, he will see that there are no monsters there. Next, they look under the bed, in the closet, and behind the toy box.

"Do you see anything, Zip?" His father asks.

Zip looks and looks. Zip sees that there are no monsters. He might be a little unsure still, but he knows that he has checked, and there are no monsters. His brain tells him so! That doesn't mean that he won't still feel scared.

And over time, now that he's done something to change his fear, his fear will begin to lessen, and he will be able to sleep!

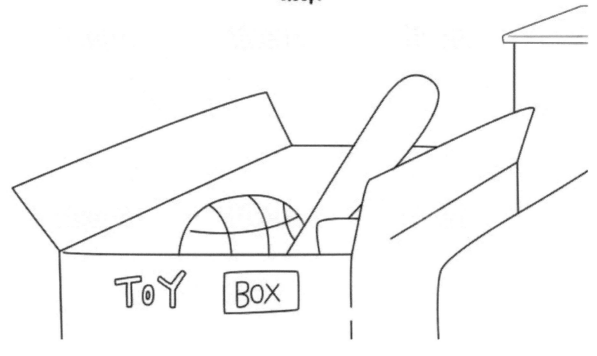

What is Zip's worst fear?

_____

Why is Zip tired?

_____

What did Zip's dad plug into his room at night?

_____

Phobias

 A phobia is a fear, but a fear that feels very, very powerful. It might make you feel terror, fear, nervous, or scared. Before you can remember, you might have a phobia, or it might come after going through something scary.

You might be afraid of flying in a plane, spiders, heights, the dark, needles, dogs, thunderstorms, or water. You could be afraid of anything. You may have a phobia now, but it does not mean that you will always be afraid of them.

Phobias Worksheet

Everyone is afraid of something. But some phobias can seem to take over and make you afraid all the time. That's why accepting your fears is important but not letting them control you. What are your fears?

Fill in the worksheet and be honest!

What makes you feel scared?

It might be airplanes, the dark, or monsters

_____

How do you handle being scared?

Do you hide? Cry? Tell someone?

_____

What happens to your body when you are scared?

Do you get shivers? Cry?

_____

What can you do next time you are scared to make yourself feel a bit better?

Could you tell someone? Make yourself laugh instead?

Distress Tolerance

What is distress tolerance?

It means how you handle something scary. Distress means being scared and worried. There are healthy ways to manage distress and not healthy ways. Below is an example of a healthy way.

Often, the terrible feelings that come with distress will lessen over time. For that to happen, you need to process your distress and what caused it.

ACCEPTS

ACCEPTS is a practice that helps change your way of thinking after distress. It stands for:

Activities - doing fun things to keep your mind off distress (playing tag)

Contributing - focusing on helping others (helping little brother with homework)

Comparisons - remember it could always be worse (it's not as bad as it could be)

Emotions - do something that makes you happy (hug your friend)

Push away - push the bad stuff away (focus on the good instead)

Thoughts - focus on your thoughts when your emotions take over (imagine something you love)

Sensations - use safe physical things to distract (your pet's warm fur)

Which of the ACCEPTS words have you used before? For example, have you used **Activity** to distract yourself?

Did it make you feel better about using ACCEPTS?

Radical Acceptance

Sometimes, things are just out of our control. Radical Acceptance means letting things be out of our control when we cannot control them ourselves. It means accepting the things we cannot change.

Write down a situation below that you cannot change. For example, someone you love got sick, or you had to move and change schools. Or maybe it's something simple like your favorite candy isn't for sale anymore.

_____

Now, write down how you felt about the thing you could not control. Did you feel scared, mad, or sad?

_____

Read the following sentence out loud. Let it sink in:

I accept that what happened was out of my control. I can not change it. It was not my fault.

When you think about what you cannot change, do you accept that it is not your fault or responsibility to change it? Circle one.

yes   no

If you said no, why?

If you said yes, great work. You've accepted that some things cannot change.

The Worry Jar

It's time to unload all of your worries! In the jar, write down everything that's been bothering you. It could be small things or big things—for example, a school test or your parent's divorce.

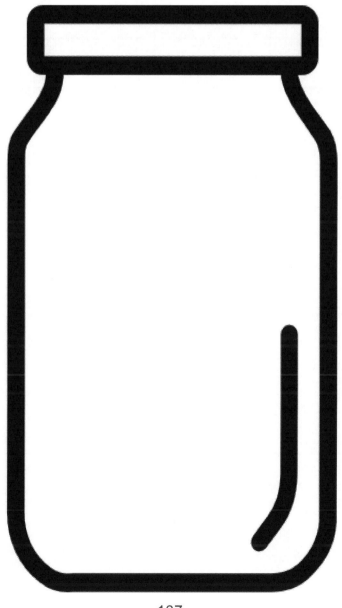

Chapter Seven: PTSD, Panic Disorder and Agoraphobia

"Every moment is a fresh beginning."

- T.S. Eliot

Tibby, the cat, had a bad day. She was riding her bike on the side of the road and didn't see a car coming around the corner. The car was coming very fast, but it swerved to miss her.

Tibby fell over on the side of the road. Her body was alright, only a scraped knee. But inside, Tibby was not alright. It really scared her. And even a week later, she would start feeling so scared, and the thought of the car would come into her mind.

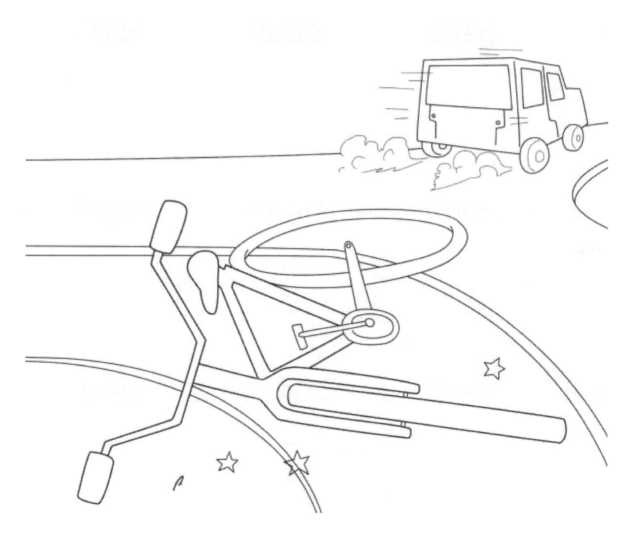

Her Mum and Dad were worried about her. They don't want her to be afraid of riding her bike forever, but they are scared, too. Her little brother Zip talks to Tibby to try to make her feel brave, reminding her that she has helped him feel brave before, too.

But the scary thoughts keep popping up in Tibby's
head at any moment. It makes her nervous and
sweaty and she feels like she can't breathe.
She hates the sight of bikes, and cars driving make
her have that instant fear.

But her Mum and Dad are going to help. They've got some
workbook pages, as well as a meeting set up with
a therapist to help Tibby feel more in control and safe.

What is Tibby the cat afraid of?

_____

Was Tibby hurt?

_____

What does Tibby not like the sight of now?

_____

Quick Assessment

Has something very scary happened to you that always left you feeling nervous?
Does seeing something that reminds you of the scary event make you feel like the event is happening all over again?
Do you have a hard time sleeping, paying attention, and staying on task because of thoughts of the scary thing that happened to you?
Do you have bad thoughts about yourself, blaming yourself for what happened?
Do your friends and the things you loved before feel less fun and like they could be taken away at any moment?
Do you always feel like there is danger everywhere and you can not relax because you have to watch out for it?
Do you often feel jumpy or like something bad could happen at any moment?

If you said yes to any of these questions, it does not always mean you have PTSD. Talk to a parent or psychiatrist.

PTSD, Panic, and Agoraphobia - What is it?

 PTSD means Post-Traumatic Stress Disorder. When something is Traumatic, it means it was scary and powerful in a bad way. Post Traumatic means how you feel after the frightening thing. When bad things happen to us, we can not just return to feeling like we did before without healing. When something terrible happens and hurts you on the inside, we have to heal just like you do when your body is hurt, and it needs time to heal and medicine.

Panic can happen in your body when you are very scared or reminded of something terrifying. It is your body's way of trying to protect you, but it does not always help in real life. Panic is when your body goes into something called Fight or Flight. This is a reaction to trauma. Your body prepares to fight the threat or run away from the danger. In a panic, your body gets itself ready by warming you up, making your heart beat faster, making your palms sweaty. It also makes you lightheaded, feel short of breath, very fearful, tremble, and have a sense that what is happening is not real.

Having a panic disorder means that these symptoms happen to you often. That makes it hard to go about your day calmly when you feel like you don't have control over your body's reactions.

Agoraphobia

This is a type of panic disorder. Agoraphobia (Ag-uh-ruh-foe-be-uh) is when someone avoids going places that make them feel scared or full of anxiety. For example, if someone has social anxiety, they will avoid places that are full of people to talk to, like school or a grocery store. Going to these places might make someone feel helpless, embarrassed, scared, sweaty, panicked, and fearful.

Self Soothe

When things are making you feel panic, it's important to have tools to help calm you. The simplest tool you have is your breathing and imagination. You can take these tools with you anywhere. No matter what else is going on, you can use breathing and imagination to soothe yourself or make yourself feel calmer and at ease and lessen the symptoms of panic. This is a skill, and you will always have it once you learn it. Follow along below to self-soothe.

Take a deep breath. Sit or lay down somewhere if you can. Feeling something solid underneath you, or even just putting your hand on something solid, can help you feel in this moment now and not in a scary place from the past. Put all your focus on your breathing, in and out, in and out. Square breathing is a good thing to use here because it makes sure that you are taking your time and breathing slowly. Getting your breath under control is very important. Once you feel like you are breathing a little easier, think of a place of total peace. It might be a quiet beach or a swing in your backyard. It might be your bed or your parent's arms. Imagine you are at that place now, safe. Comfortable. Calm. Happy. This place is always there for you, always ready to make you feel peaceful and safe. You can stay there as long as you need.

Emotion Regulation

Emotion Regulation is when you can manage your emotions in a good way. It means you can calm yourself when you are upset and cheer yourself up when you are sad. It's balancing out your feelings so that you do not feel like you are all over the place with your emotions.

When you cannot use emotional regulation, it can look like a temper tantrum or a screaming fight. With anxiety, it can be challenging to use emotional regulation. That's why it's good to practice using it.

Slowing down and choosing your reaction, rather than letting your emotions and feelings choose for you, is how emotional regulation works.

Fill in the bubbles below with things that make you panic or feel out of control of your emotions. You might need some emotional regulation. An example might be: Being on the subway platform and being in the subway car.

Some things you could do to lessen anxiety and fear over these places could be:

- **Use Dragon's Breath** - push out a big breath, starting from low in your belly. Imagine it's made of fire, and it's burning away all the fear and anxiety you feel. Blow out for four seconds.
- **Use a self-soothing activity** by breathing deeply and imagining a place that makes you feel safe and happy, like your room.
- **Take a mindful body scan** - Relax every part of your body as you think about it, moving from one body part to another, and relax all muscles.

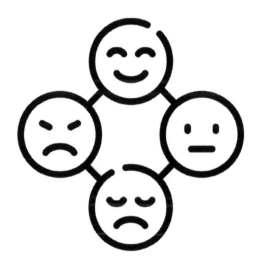

Stop, Look, Listen

Take a seat somewhere comfortable. This activity is all about slowing down and noticing what is around you. Sit quietly for a few minutes and fill in the blank spaces below.

What do you hear? Maybe a car, a bird chirping, a sibling?

_____

What do you see? Maybe a tree, a toy, or a pencil?

_____

What do you taste? Maybe water, a snack, or nothing?

_____

What do you touch? Maybe your chair, your clothes, the sofa?

_____

What do you smell? Maybe a snack, the grass, or a pet?

_____

Chapter Eight: OCD, Compulsive Behaviours and Body-Focused Repetitive Behaviours

"Go easy on yourself. Whatever you do today, let it be enough."

-Unknown

Zip the Cat loves to do things a certain way.
When he gets dressed, he likes to put his left arm
in his shirt first, then his right, then his head. He
feels like he has to always make his bed with the
pillows placed just perfectly in the middle.

When Zip leaves his room, he turns out the light, and then flicks it back on again, before turning it off for real. He's not really sure why, but he wants to make sure that the light is really off.

Zip's family knows how he likes to do certain things. He taps his feet twice on the doormat, no more, no less. If anything touches his face on one side, he has to let it touch his face on the other side, too. Zip doesn't really know why he feels the need to do these things, but he feels that he must, that if he doesn't, something bad might happen.

His Mum and Dad talk to him about it. They tell him that nothing bad will happen if he doesn't do his taps and touches, but also that they understand that Zip has a Compulsive Disorder.

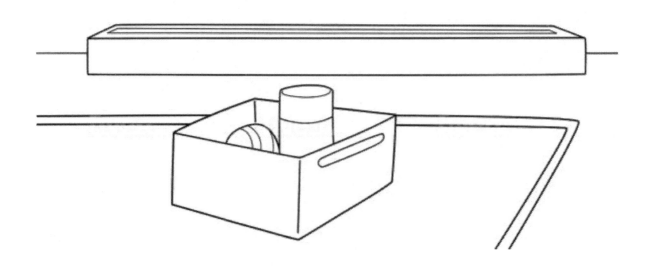

How does Zip like to put on his shirt?

How many times does Zip need to turn off the light?

What does Zip think will happen if he doesn't do these things?

Quick Assessment

Obsessions

Do you...

- *Worry about germs and getting sick?*
- *Feel things have to be just right, or will something terrible happen?*
- *Have scary thoughts that you do not want to have?*
- *Fear about doing something wrong?*

Compulsions

Do you...

- *Check things twice, three times, four times...?*
- *Do a task over and over until it's 'right'?*
- *Worry that something bad will happen if you don't do something unrelated?*
- *Think about something over and over again?*

If you said yes to the questions above, it does not always mean you have OCD. Talk to a parent or a psychiatrist.

What is OCD?

 *OCD is Obsessive Compulsive Disorder.* An *Obsession* is when you cannot stop thinking about or doing something, even when you might not want to anymore. Compulsion is when you feel like you have to do something; a repetitive movement or task or something bad will usually happen. It could be counting something over and over or not being able to stop thinking one thought over and over.

You can have compulsions, obsessions, or both. It becomes Obsessive Compulsive Disorder when it takes up much of your time, such as more than an hour of your day, or when it interferes with the rest of your regular life.

Body-Focused Repetitive Behaviours

Body-Focused Repetitive Behaviours are a group of behaviors. You are repeatedly doing something to your body because of anxiety. These behaviors can include nail-biting, hair pulling, scratching at the skin, and many others.

What causes OCD and Body-Focused Repetitive Behaviours?

These disorders and behaviors happen partly because of genetics. Maybe someone in your family also has similar behaviors. But it's also thought that OCD and Body-Focused Repetitive Behaviours can come about because of stressful situations.

The OCD Monster

This is your OCD monster. It likes to tell you what to do. It can be a bit bossy, can't it? Below, write in the bubbles your OCD monster makes you do. For example, counting your shoes repeatedly because you're worried you might fail a test.

Obsession   **Compulsion**

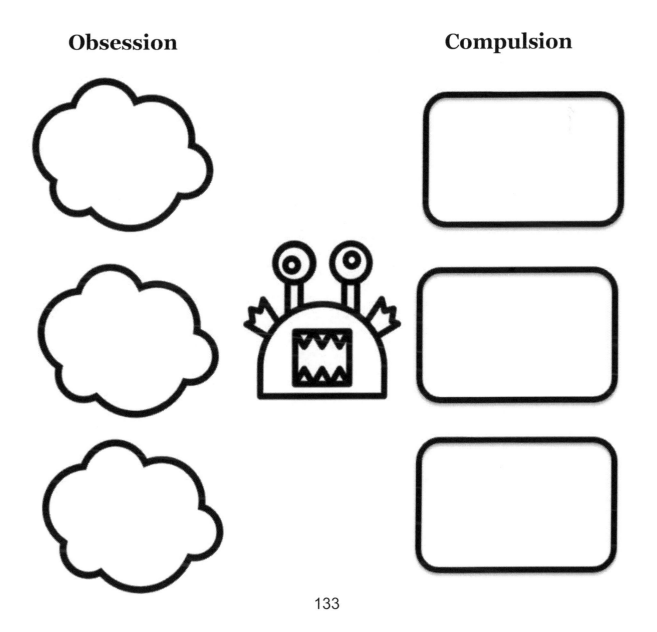

What would happen if you don't do what the OCD monster wants you to? Do you feel like something terrible might happen?

Thought —> Action

Fill in the chart. On one side, write down your thoughts or urges. On the other side, write a DBT action you could take instead of completing the urge/thought.

Thought/Urge	DBT Action
flicking on/off lights	Stop and take 3 deep breaths

Matching

Draw a line between each symbol on the left and its matching pair on the right.
The first one is done as an example.

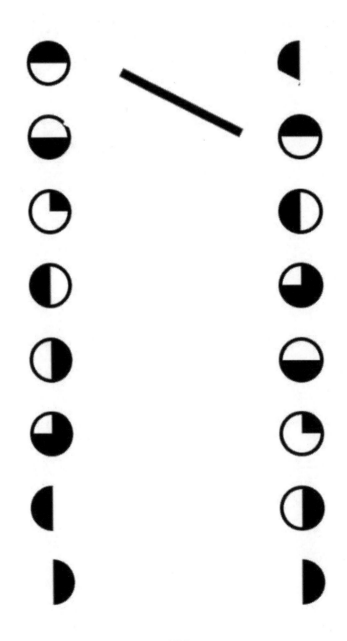

Chapter Nine: Selective Mutism

"Nothing is permanent in this wicked world, not even our troubles."

-Charlie Chaplin

Tibby the cat can sometimes lose her voice.
It is not because her throat is sore or she's sick.
It's because sometimes she gets too worried
and anxious to talk.

Tibby is fine talking at home, or around her friends at the park. But when it comes to talking in class, she is less comfortable. In fact, she has begun to find that it is next to impossible. The feeling only grew worse and worse until Tibby was so scared and anxious that she was not able to talk while at school at all.

Her teacher noticed that Tibby was no longer speaking at school at all, and so she talked to Tibby and her parents to try to find ways to make Tibby feel more comfortable at school. If they could figure out what was making her so worried, they might be able to help.

It was quiet in the classroom after all the
other kids had left. Though Tibby didn't say
anything herself, she found that she was more
comfortable when she had some quiet time,
and it wasn't the classroom herself that was
scary but being around a large number
of classmates for the whole school day that
made her nervous.

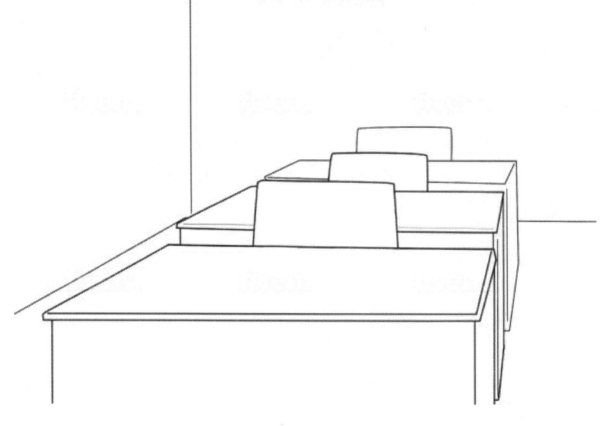

Tibby and her teacher and parents agreed that
it might help Tibby if she was able to get some
quiet time to herself a few times a day.

Where did Tibby feel too nervous to talk?

_____

What made Tibby nervous?

_____

What solution did Tibby, her teacher, and her parents come up with?

_____

Quick Assessment

When you are in a certain place, do you often feel...

- Like you don't want to talk or visit anyone?
- Feel safest when you are quiet?
- Feel like your words won't come out, right?
- Have no idea what to say?
- Get very nervous that you won't say the right thing?
- Worry that people will make fun of you for speaking?
- Feel unconnected to what's going on around you?

If you answered yes to the questions above, it does not always mean you have selective mutism. Talk to a parent or psychiatrist.

What is Selective mutism?

If you feel like you cannot speak in certain places because you are too scared and nervous, you might have selective mutism. Mutism means being unable to speak. Selective means that you choose when and for how long. You might be comfortable and happy to talk to your friends at their houses or your siblings at home. But maybe you get too nervous about opening your mouth at the grocery store. You might also begin to feel uncomfortable speaking anywhere at all.

This can make it hard to make new friends or keep hanging out with your current friends. It can be tough to go about your day when you are so worried and stressed that it is not good for your health. It can make being successful at school very hard, and though it is not common, it can be awful for someone going through this.

Remember, it's okay to feel scared or worried. There is nothing wrong with you if you are nervous about talking in front of people. But to make your life easier, and, most importantly, to get rid of that scary uneasy feeling, you have to work on your anxiety. Practicing to lessen your anxiety will make you feel lighter and less scared.

What makes you nervous?

Below, write or draw what makes you too nervous to talk. It could be being at school or seeing strangers. What are you afraid will happen if you do speak?

What do you think would make it easier for you to speak?

For example, maybe it would help to imagine your classmates as more silly and not so scary- what if they were all wearing funny costumes?

Telephone

A great way to make you feel comfortable in a place with people is to get better at being around people. Remember, Interpersonal Effectiveness can help with that.

Grab a few friends. It can be parents, siblings, friends, or anyone.

This game is all about talking. And the best part is: you can't say the wrong thing. In fact, it's kind of more fun if you do say the wrong thing!

This is the game of the telephone. Sitting in a circle, the person who starts whispers a sentence into their neighbor's ear very quietly. Then, that person turns to the person on their other side and whispers what they think they heard. It goes on like this until the whisper comes all the way back to the original whisperer. The original whisperer will listen to the sentence and then say what they heard aloud. Often, the original sentence and the end sentence will be very different! That's what happens when it goes through several people.

Remember, the great thing about this game is:

1. It's quiet
2. There is no wrong thing to say
3. It's fun
4. You get to practice talking around others without some of the stress of talking normally or outside of the game.

Dare List

It can be scary to do things that make us worried or scared. Sometimes, all it takes is adding a little fun to make it less scary. Below is a dare list! If you can check off this list, you are getting closer and closer to not letting these things scare you anymore. Be brave, and have fun!

I dare you to...

1. Say "Hi" to someone you know but haven't spoken to before. You don't have to say anything else, just "Hi!"
2. Ask someone if they're having a good day. You don't have to say anything else after that unless you want to.
3. Next time someone asks you a question, answer it and then ask them one. Maybe their favorite color or ice cream.
4. Find something you like about a person. Maybe their t-shirt or their laugh. Tell them.

Chapter Ten: For Parents

Getting Involved

 The most important thing you can do for your child is to be understanding and present for them. Your child's needs are unique to them, and as their parent, you are the best person to help guide them to the skills and tools that can help make their lives easier.

Being a supportive parent is a full-time job. But making sure that your child's foundational skills are being created now means that later on in your child's life, they will be able to handle better the challenges and trials they meet because they will already have a sturdy base of skills and a support system to back them.

Validation

Teaching your child self-validation is key. Showing them that each individual matters and deserves to take up space helps confidence and self-worth. Watching the language you use about yourself around your child can help shape them to see themselves, too, as worthy subconsciously. Children notice positivity and treat themselves with kindness and respect because how we talk and treat ourselves is molded into how we approach the world. Being an example of self-worth and confidence helps your child to see themselves that way, too.

Giving yourself validation for the trials you have endured brings peace and self-acceptance. It's a gift to help teach your child these skills.

Validating your child as a parent is also important. Acknowledging that their unique abilities, skills, and attributes shape who they are and what they bring to the world makes them feel validated. Approval or simply just acceptance from parents is a huge step toward having self-confidence and helps heal anxiety in children significantly.

Positive and Negative Behaviours

As said above, your behaviors, reactions, and self-image all help to shape your child's, as well. Being a positive, supportive, healthy example for your child can mean a world of difference.

Pessimism can be tough to shake, but choosing to look to the brighter side of things can significantly shape your child's attitude. The difference between a bad day and a good day can be as simple as choosing to rise above the bad things that happened, maybe the things you cannot control, and making the most of the good things you can handle. Celebrate the small victories, and be your child's champion. Tell them when you're proud of them, even if it's only a small achievement. Small things add up and up until they become the big things.

Learning the skills for yourself might be an asset when helping your child learn these skills. Below is a short suggested activity for each of the main skills.

Mindfulness

Meditation is healing for everyone. Close your eyes and go to a place where you feel calm and unbothered. Breathe deeply and slowly. Feel the tensions start to drain away, like bathwater down a drain. You are left only with tranquillity and relaxation.

Interpersonal Effectiveness

Try talking to someone while being fully engaged with them. It's okay to be nervous. Make eye contact while they speak. Nod, offer your thoughts. Don't just hear, but listen well.

Distress Tolerance

Breathe deeply if it makes you nervous. Feel your feet planted on the solid floor to feel grounded. You are alright, safe, and in this moment now, but this moment will pass just like all the others.

Emotion Regulation

Notice what you are feeling. Notice how your body reacts and how your mind reacts. Acknowledge it. Accept it. This reaction is unchangeable, and that's okay. Accept it, and let it go, let it move on.

Getting Help

Don't forget that there is nothing wrong with getting help. In fact, it is the best way to ensure that the things you pass on to your child are only the good things. As we grow up, we carry our childhood traumas and issues. Sometimes, it seems that they are simply a part of us. While it is true that the experiences are a part of us, the behavior from the trauma and the lasting hurt they might have are not. Getting help means taking the lessons and lessening the pain.

Activities you can do with your child.....

Mental Health Walks

Take your child out on a daily mental health walk. It can be five or thirty minutes up and down the road or through a huge park.

Not only does a walk with you give your child a space to bring up anything they might want to talk to you about, but it is also refreshing and mentally stimulating for them. Get them to point out things they notice—funny clouds, changing leaves, cute dogs or interesting people. You can make a game of it, as well. Look for everything of a particular color, or play a word game. Best yet, talk about how they're feeling. It can be a great space to share and grow a trusting bond. Not to mention, walks will also give you both fresh air and exercise, which are great for mental health.

Parent/child night

It can be tough to make sure you spend quality time together between work, school, activities, jobs, friends, and other commitments. Have a parent/child night every once in a while (periodically is best). Plan it ahead, and spend even an hour together doing something relaxing or stress relieving. It could be a puzzle or game night, a movie date, a spa day, a picnic, or something slightly less structured, like building forts or playing in the snow. Give your child your undivided attention at this time. No phones, no other distractions. Just play and relaxation for both of you.

Final Thoughts

DBT therapies are quiet, thoughtful, and safe ways to help cope with anxiety. They actively work to take control of your emotions, reactions, and body to make you feel better and more at ease.

Taking the time to practice the skills in this workbook will help lessen the bad feelings of anxiety, worry, and stress. Actively taking charge of your body's reactions puts you back in control, not your anxiety.

Some important things to remember:

- There is nothing wrong with you
- You are not doing anything wrong
- You are capable of far more than you know
- You are stronger than you feel
- Anxiety does not control you
- You are doing well, just as you are at this moment

Next Steps: If this workbook helped you, that's fantastic! Learning about yourself and how your mind and body work are never done. As you grow and change, new challenges and things to learn are always around the corner.

Talking to a therapist or a counselor can help when you feel like you might need some guidance.

When in doubt, talk it out with someone you love and trust.

Review Request

If you enjoyed this book or found it useful...

I'd like to ask you for a quick favor:

Please share your thoughts and leave a quick REVIEW. Your feedback matters and helps me make improvements to provide the best books possible.

Reviews are so helpful to both readers and authors, so any help would be greatly appreciated.

You can leave a review below.

https://tinyurl.com/dbt-kids-review

Also, please join my ARC team to get early access to my releases.

https://barretthuang.com/arc-team/

Thank you!

Further Reading

Boundaries Workbook for Kids

Fun, Educational & Age-Appropriate Lessons About Personal Safety & Consent | Learn to Set Healthy Body Boundaries at Home, School, & Online
(For Ages 8-12)

Get your copy here:

https://tinyurl.com/Boundaries-Workbook-for-Kids

DBT Workbook For Teens:

A Complete Dialectical Behavior Therapy Toolkit

Essential Coping Skills and Practical Activities To Help Teenagers & Adolescents Manage Stress, Anxiety, ADHD, Phobias & More

Get your copy here:

https://tinyurl.com/dbt-teens

DBT Workbook for Adults

Develop Emotional Wellbeing with Practical Exercises for Managing Fear, Stress, Worry, Anxiety, Panic Attacks, Intrusive Thoughts & More

(Includes 12-Week Plan for Anxiety Relief)

Get your copy here:

https://tinyurl.com/dbtadult

About the Author

Barrett Huang is an author and businessman. Barrett spent years discovering the best ways to manage his OCD, overcome his anxiety, and learn to embrace life. Through his writing, he hopes to share his knowledge with readers, empowering people of all backgrounds with the tools and strategies they need to improve their mental wellbeing and be happy and healthy.

When not writing or running his business, Barrett loves to spend his time studying. He majored in Psychology and completed the DBT skills certificate course taught by Dr. Marsha Linehan. Barrett's greatest inspiration is the legendary Bruce Lee, who said, "The key to immortality is first living a life worth remembering."

https://barretthuang.com/

Resources

Here are a few resources you might want to check out for more information.

Anxiety Canada

Parent and Child resources

https://www.anxietycanada.com/articles/parent-child/

The Child Mind Institute

Anxiety in Children

https://childmind.org/topics/anxiety/

The Child Mind Institute

Dialectical Behavior Therapy

https://childmind.org/article/dbt-dialectical-behavior-therapy

Coping Skills for Kids

Calming Anxiety

https://copingskillsforkids.com/calming-anxiety

Made in United States
Troutdale, OR
11/17/2024